THE ART (

MARKO DA COSTA

MW01288517

NORTH OAK

& PAGES

the art of feeling © 2018 by Marko Da Costa. All rights reserved.
Printed in Canada. No part of this book may be used or reproduced
in any form or means without permission in writing from the
publisher, except for the inclusion of brief quotations in a review.

Published by North Oak & Pages
706 The Queensway
Toronto, Ontario M8Y 1L3

www.markodacosta.com

Cover Design: Joshua Scott
Book Layout: Marko Da Costa
Editor: Carly Brennan

ISBN-13:978-1717268372
ISBN-10:1717268374

AUTHOR

to my mother and father
kimberley francis and phillip james
thank you
for breathing life into
an instrument
that is now ready
to play
its melody

-

to my grandmother
elaine hirst
without you
I would be nothing

-

to the love of my life
omar senan
without you
this book would not be as complete
thank you for the inspiration
your love
is truly profound

-

to areej abu-ali
thank you
for introducing me
to my inner poet

I dedicate this book to
my siblings
michael hirst
mariah james
brittany mcdermid
tavon james
jeniya colbourne
jayda francis

let this book
be a map
whenever your spirits
feel lost or alone

     –

I would like to also
dedicate this book to
anyone out there
seeking sanctuary
from the ways
of this world
rest your worries
in these pages
your voice
has been heard

EULOGY
(the preface)

my deepest condolences to the old
me
may you forever rest in peace

on behalf of the man I used to be
I would like to thank everyone who
found their way to these pages
today
to celebrate the life of a man
who was forever searching for
himself
in other people and other places
collecting pieces of his spirit
and giving them away as charity
to those who took and never gave
and also sharing a place in time
with those who taught him
the meaning of passion and love

as a child
he was born with
the burden of reality
and as you all may know
at times we forget
how cruel this world can be
and that the loneliest place
sometimes happens to be
right inside
each and every one of us

that shadow that follows
our every step
that voice that mocks
our very existence
those feelings that wrap us up
in emotional distance
separating us from
connecting
with one another

over the years
I've come to learn
that you can't blame
a man for doing wrong
when wrong is all
he ever knew

do we punish
a bird that cannot fly

if from birth
the world
confines the bird
to a cage

I want you all to understand
that the man I used to be
never suffered
when his time came

you see, even though
there were times
he felt lost and alone
there were many times when
he laughed
he loved
he smiled
he danced
he sung
and felt
like he finally belonged

there's not a thing
he would have changed
because in his last hours
he softly whispered to me
that he lived a good life

but I'm not here today
to mourn the loss
of my old friend
I'm here today
to celebrate the life
he sacrificed
in order to give me
a better one

and here I stand
thankful
for change
and thankful
for growth
cause all I needed
was release from
sorrow
in order to understand
love
and the room for
acceptance
in order to find
peace

without the old me
I wouldn't have
been able to
experience this journey
in finding myself
through inner peace

I promise you
this is not goodbye
we'll reunite again
in another place
and another time

TABLE OF CONTENTS

SORROW

Sorrow is the unwanted house guest that sometimes
overstays its welcome. No matter how many times we
tell ourselves that one day we'll find the courage to tell
sorrow never to return, we somehow always leave the door
wide open with the welcome mat laid out but there comes a
point when we must respect our home and change
the locks for good.

don't be afraid to face the breakdown
breaking down is the first step to starting over

BREAKDOWN

you used to call me honey
sweet and delicious
when summer days
were long
and lust
was fresher
than a glass
of lemonade
on a hot afternoon

but summer
doesn't last forever
does it

tell me...

did his lips taste like honey
did his touch comfort you
when the leaves changed colours

bees must know patience my dear
how will they build if not in harmony

maybe one day you'll come to learn that
nectar doesn't turn into honey overnight
and not all honey satisfies the soul

HONEY

I asked you
what made you cheat on me

you said to me
you made me

but that's impossible

so I then asked you
do the dandelions
force the bees
to take pollen from
other flowers or trees

TAKE RESPONSIBILITY

when you went down on him
did he look into your eyes
and see all of the hard work
I put into that soul

was it ryan
chris
or nathan

justin
kevin
or maybe jason

honestly
I've lost count
and my mind
is tired of
trying to pretend

if this wasn't really love
why did you make it
feel so real then

WHY DID YOU PRETEND

for your own safety, I pray by now
that you've fled for the mountains
cause the earth is about to crumble
as I make my way towards you
and the flames from my rage
are about to incinerate your ego
right out of existence
no need for an apology
you've already made your bed
so, at this point, you might as well
lay down another one of your sleazy tricks
and after I smash every window
out of your sports car
don't come crying to me
why don't you go cry on the shoulder of
your insurance company
cause I'm taking everything
when I leave your world
so say goodbye to the sun
that once brought you warmth
kiss the oceans farewell
they'll no longer be washing you of your filth
watch as they dry up, the moment I vanish
so I advise you to ask your illicit lover
to help you pick up the pieces after I'm gone
since the two of you share a special place
together in hell
so long and good riddance
you played yourself
and now all you have is eternity
to think about
who the f*ck
you thought you
were dealing with

HELL HATH NO FURY

we built something so beautiful
that you gave away
my spirit broke
when he called to confess that day
your knees bruised
weeping for me not to walk away
so I washed you of your sins that night
baptized you of his name
and even though the pain was unbearable
I found it in my heart to stay
cause even the angels cried
when our sandcastles washed away

SANDCASTLES WE BUILT TOGETHER

it was supposed to be one harmless dance

you offered to buy me a drink
and then asked me for my name
I tried to avoid you
I belonged to someone else
but you were persistent
and I was weak to your charm
the mystery in your eyes
and the challenge in your smile
drew me closer
you temporarily filled the void
in my gloomy love story
a story shared between
my current lover and I
a feeling I longed for
an easy escape from reality

so we danced the night away

and in that moment
I knew there was no turning back

I became yours as I strayed from him
the regretful path I selfishly followed
and will forever regret

my firm grip around this gun
the gun that you gave to me
lately I've been under the influence of pain
the pain we've both caused ourselves
and here we are
face to face
ready to lose it all
click one – empty
is it you or is it him
is it me or is it them
what's it going to be
now take the gun - place it in your mouth
and let's see if they're going to save you now
click two – empty
just like the promises you told me
go ahead, pass the gun
I've got some secrets to confess this time
click three – should have been me
infidelity is a game of snakes and ladders
and we're always trying to climb higher
so naïve to the lies of the serpents
click four – lucky you
one round left
guess you're finally free of me
so I place the gun against my temple
click five – how am I still alive
could love be this foolish
to allow two fools like us to survive
to kill the hearts of those next in line

LOVERS' ROULETTE

god doesn't make toys
for your pleasure

he didn't make me
so that when you grow bored
you could just break me

I whisper into your ear
I love you

words I've been meaning to confess
but too afraid to say

you respond with just a smile that says
I care for you
but it's only temporary

I told you
that I was on my way
headed in your direction
towards loyal boulevard
you promised me
that you would meet me
but you never showed
telling me that I move too slow
guess I should have
caught all the stop signs
and flashing red lights
accusing me of shifty driving
when it's always been you
breaking all the rules
late night drives
undercover passengers
like I'm not intelligent enough
to check my blind spots
and since you're headed up
a one way street
I'm sitting here
trying to figure out
how to make this u turn
while my trust is parked
somewhere out on
middle of nowhere avenue

MIDDLE OF NOWHERE AVENUE

why are you always
there when I am here
and here when I am there

near when I am far
and far when I am near

Friday morning
songs about love through my earphones
as I commute to work
fantasizing about all that love
has out there for me
- yearning

Friday night
I put the effort in to look appealing
bourbon on the rocks
gay bar with the boys
then there was you
our eyes meet
you ask me for my number
I don't object
- curiosity

Saturday morning
I wake to your text
dinner at five you ask
I smile as I bite my lip
it's been awhile since
the sun has felt this warm
- excitement

Saturday night
middle eastern food
my favorite
you paid attention
we exchange hilarious stories
you pay the bill and drive me home
you don't ask to come upstairs but instead
when will I see you again
I smile... tomorrow
- wanting more but playing it cool

Sunday morning
I wait around all day
for your text
four in the afternoon
like you forgot the plans
you tell me to be ready by six
how quickly you're forgiven
and how quickly I forget
- tricks of the trade

Sunday night
this time it's seafood
shared memories of your childhood
how you're forever searching for love like me
those eyes become a trap with no exit
I fall deeper
it's unhealthy but I don't fight it
- I give you my trust

Monday morning
I try my hardest not to text you
but lust takes dominion over
everything I tell myself
I stand for
I text you
are you free tonight
- needing

Monday night
your hands caress my thighs
as you enter me
breaking down the wall
I worked so hard to build
I become yours
not knowing
that you don't become mine
- one sided

Tuesday morning
one text with empty promises
that we'll hang again sometime soon
was I wrong for believing in you
- naïve

Tuesday night
I try to busy myself
with positive thoughts of you and I
but I slip up and reach out for your affection
let's hang tonight
but you gutted me with your response
can't I'm busy
- you went for the kill

Wednesday night
I touch myself
to the thoughts of you
hoping to remember
what it feels like to feel wanted
    -   I lose myself

Thursday morning
I sit staring at my office wall
I spiral into my insecurities
    -   no missed calls

Thursday night
I never go out on weeknights
tonight's different
something tells me to go out
I find you at the bar
not as busy as you claimed
but busy enough to occupy your time
on the lips of another
    -   you took the warmth of the sun with you

Friday morning
I commute to work
songs about what it could have been
    -   loneliness

Friday night
I put the effort in to look appealing
bourbon on the rocks
gay bar with the boys
repeat cycle
    -   the human condition

oceans of emotions
and mountains of pride

miles apart
in this king bed

as we lay
side by side

OCEANS OF PRIDE

I am the sun
you are the moon

two lovers
forever
worlds apart

STAR CROSSED LOVERS

it's like we're trapped in time
stuck on a constant loop

our feelings for each other
held hostage by our egos

communication the ransom
but we're unwilling to pay

HOSTAGE

I tried to shape you into the *perfect lover*
selfishly cutting pieces of you out of existence
folding and folding over things I cannot change

ORIGAMI

it's okay for a man to cry

when a man cries
his heart is making music

a vulnerable tempo
calling out for
a patient listener
to sway with

you once told me
that I was worth
a million miles

nowadays all you do
is complain about
how much your feet hurt

A MILLION MILES

to be yours
you wanted me
to move mountains
swim the deepest seas
turn water into wine

but I'm not a god
I'm just human
and all I have to offer
is exactly what you see

TAKE IT OR LEAVE IT

you call me to tell me
that you just want to be friends

but ripping out a still beating heart
isn't how a friendship begins

LET'S JUST BE FRIENDS

yesterday
I saw you with him
and in my mind
I shattered
the two of you
into a million pieces
so that
I didn't have to face
the fact that
my reflection
no longer
existed in your world

I've been drinking all night
I drink of you
like a bottle of bourbon
down to the last drop
my mind cloudy
the vision of self-respect blurry
so I lay here
in the middle
of my living room floor
spinning out of control
losing consciousness
allowing my insecurities
to intoxicate me
when the morning comes
I feel sick
disgusted in the fact
that I allowed you inside of me
I throw you up
begging for mercy
and after the day passes me by
it's you that I call again
parched for affection
thirsty for attention

DRUNK OFF INSECURITIES

I allow you to
stay the night
but by the time
morning comes
you're already gone
and you've taken
my self-esteem with you

THIEF IN THE NIGHT

and even though
we're in the same bed
my heart
sleeps alone
tonight

MY HEART SLEEPS ALONE

there was a moment in time
when I lost myself
I wept five days straight
as I tarnished my holy temple
bathed my spirit in lust
and crucified my righteousness
all in the name of
finding myself
in a sea of wanderers
so I prayed
that my tears would
wash away my sins
and that I would be freed
from the lies of the devil

LOST AT SEA

my heart
is not some cheap motel
where you can
leave your baggage
kick up your feet
and come and go as you please

I could have killed you that morning when you selfishly decided to break up with me on my birthday. I wasn't sure if I should have been celebrating my birth or the death of our relationship in that moment. Why would you light up my emotions only to blow them out in front of me? Tease me with a cake that never belonged to me in the first place? It was always your cake and you sat there with a smirk on your face as you ate it too. F**king clown. I should have caused a scene. I should have cracked that champagne bottle against your forehead. Toasted to my freedom. But that's then and this is now, and like they say, *they all come back around.* And around you came. Telling me *I still love you,* but hold on - didn't want me then so tell me why you want me now? Not a damn thing has changed. Or maybe it's the fact that the streets have been talking and you've heard I've been kicking it with karma. Trust me I feel no way of introducing the two of you. I've told him about all of the nights I'd wait up at home for you or all the other men I had to share you with. Karma says he's excited to meet you and that it's overdue. Guess you'll never see me again in my birthday suit. Now every year my birthday comes around I'm reminded of how I dodged that bullet and that the best gift you ever gave me was self-respect.

Thank you.

the promises we once made
now galaxies apart
where have they gone
who have we become

we're falling
slowly crumbling
and I'm beginning
to feel like the end is near
let's face the truth
we can't keep this up
it's becoming a disaster
just give in
and let's let this thing go
we'll let it fall
like the london bridge

LONDON BRIDGE IS FALLING DOWN

I'm out here in deep waters
waiting for you to rescue me
I'm slowly drowning
watching you go through
the motions of you and I
but you're too afraid
to get your feet wet
too afraid to swim
through these emotions
to meet me halfway
and I'm desperately
reaching out to you
slowly fading
into memories
can't you see
your boyfriend
is drifting away

DRIFTING AWAY

there's no happiness
in the sunsets
that wait for me

why did you leave
sunshine

FAREWELL SUNSHINE

some days I felt like I knew who I was
others I felt I was still searching for myself

your love made me feel like a prince
you always wanted to give me the world and so much more
but sometimes the drama made me feel like a therapist
you'd tell me you were sick and tired of my sh*t
and on those nights I was your doctor
nursing you back to wanting me again
you swore I was your angel sent from heaven
a teacher well versed in the ways of love
your guide to a deeper connection
the model of your purpose
but that never lasted
I accounted for every time we swore we were done
a teller banking all the hurtful words we shared
even though we never meant them
the damage was already done
and god knows I'm not the best at home repair
and on the last day of summer
I said goodbye like your favorite camp counsellor
cause after all the things I thought I was
I came to realize the one thing I wasn't
was your soulmate

nights alone in this house
chill me to the bone
distant memories of us
have been haunting me lately
objects of yours vanish on their own
the pictures of us that hang from the walls
now stare at me with dread
there must be something evil here
cause I hear your voice call out to me
but when I run towards your cries
there's no one there
why does this entity taunt me so
I must have done something
unimaginably wicked to deserve this
even when I drift into a deep sleep
nightmares of spending eternity
in this state of loneliness
sit heavy on my chest
the old hag here to deliver regret
and I can't seem to shake
this phantom draft
a deep coldness in my heart
it's only when morning
comes to my rescue
that I come to realize
you were there all along
and it was I
who was never there
cause the only thing haunted
about this place
is me

HAUNTED

this gravity is pulling us apart
and if we don't open our minds
we're just two souls
on a galactic journey to nowhere

and you keep pulling me back
interrupting the universe and its signs

don't you realize that we need
a moment to find peace of mind

understand that the answers to our future
are out in space and time

SPACE AND TIME

that night
a quarter past three
I walked for hours on end
with nowhere in mind
miles away from home
I found the loneliest river
and sat in it
eventually I lost track of time
staring at the fireflies
I cried my eyes out
my mind covered in bruises
I was trembling and exhausted
I had just fought with the decision
and it beat me to near death
so I listened to the heartbroken tune
of the crying cicadas
as the water washed away
the debris of our complacency
from under my nails
that's when
I let reality sink in...

I'm a murderer

I had just ended the life
of our relationship

MURDERER

you gently took my hand
as you led me into the woods

and even though
we were side by side
I felt alone that day

with despair in our eyes
we watched the flowers
say their final goodbyes

as I cried
they began to
wither and die

END OF THE AFFAIR

I cried all night
and in the morning
my spirit
was cleansed of you

SPIRITUAL CLEANSING

you promised me
we would grow a garden
out of our goals and aspirations
but I guess nothing ever bloomed

the seeds we sow together
can't just grow on their own
and all I've been doing lately
is crying
wishing these tears
would miraculously
bring these flowers to life

but you lack the skills
to understand the beauty
of growth

and don't take it personally
but I've come to realize
our garden's pointless
now that I've outgrown you

DON'T TAKE IT PERSONALLY

LOVE

Just like food, filling your house with the right kind of love
will nourish and help your home to grow healthy and strong.
Love is essential to every room in your home. Without it,
your house will gradually come undone.

how many days and nights
did he leave your heart begging
for mercy in a desert so dry

did he watch in joy
while you struggled
to lift yourself up again
with the wings he clipped

it hurts to know that you felt alone
in the last hours of a dying love

reaching out for answers
from an apparition
who was never really there

my mother use to tell me
that I had the power
to raise love back from the dead
white magic drawn from the roots
of the compassion that lives within

I know you feel like your heart
will never find its way again
but if you come with me
I promise you
I can breathe life
back into your lonely bones

POWER OF RESURGENCE

he opens up
doors
inside of me
that I never
even knew
existed

DOORS

I sit here
in this coffee shop
wishing you knew
who I was
or even my name
so badly I want to confess
but society
keeps my mouth shut
and the thought
of embarrassing you
challenges my confidence
men shouldn't like men
what if that's always
been your train of thought
so I look away
and hope one day
you'll join me
at this lonely table
and ask me for my name

BOY IN THE COFFEE SHOP

word of mouth is
that you've been telling
your boys that
you're into me

open your ears
and listen carefully
just maybe you'll hear
the sound of my heartbeat

place your hand
on my chest
do you feel that feeling
that would be mutuality

and I swear
I don't mean to be nosey
but I can smell
your undeniable lust for me

if you clear your vision
you'll come to see
what I see

so I'll just confess
when I'm with you
all five senses tell me
that you're
the one for me

ALL FIVE SENSES

it's your smooth
personality
charm
and masculinity
that had me fall
head over sneakers
for you

long days at the beach
we'd skip school
make out sessions
in the back
of your dad's cadillac
soft serve ice cream
low cut chucks
hubba bubba love
late night horror flicks

this is what
summer love is

as the sun sets
on this busy city
I call out to you
to light up
this lonely heart of mine
your affection
moves me in so many ways
physics never could
and this chemistry
between you and I
unbreakable
car horns and sirens
I've held up traffic
cause this thing we have
is an emergency
pressing matters
to have you inside of me
we can't deny the urgency
city full of voices
just follow the sound
of my heartbeat
directions to a playground
of profound love
time is of the essence
so just detour through
the tunnel vision
and ignore the distractions
there you'll find
that I belong to you
in this city of undeniable attraction

CITY OF UNDENIABLE ATTRACTION

I'm elegant like fine china
fragile at times
handle me with care
a treasure
I promise you'll find

FINE CHINA

the waters of your river
keep me afloat
while I aimlessly wade
through you
it's the patience of your flow
that calms my stride
it's the promise of your tide
to wash away the past
and clear my mind
and I know you tell me
that there's no need to hide
that all you have
is patience and time
but it's the fear
of drowning in you
whenever I get déjà vu

DÉJÀ VU

kiss me so softly
let your lips
whisper to me
the most beautiful
love story of time

my insecurities are an endless fashion show
but you become the designer of my confidence

THE PERFECT TAILOR

I seek solace in your love
will you open up when I come knocking

I long for your fingers
to play me like a piano
the way you gracefully play
the greatest love songs
of Frédéric Chopin

A CLASSICAL LOVE STORY

one

    step

        at

           a

              time

                  my

                      love

                          patience

THE ART OF PATIENCE

I am no walk in the park
nor the birds that hum so gently

I am the terrain of complicated paths
and the refreshing river
that awaits you at the end

JOURNEY TO FIND ME

the flowers
refused to bloom
until you were finally ready
to confess your love for me

what's more relaxing
than the sound of rain drops
tap dancing against my window
while I float so calmly in your arms
letting time escape us

SUNDAY MORNINGS

I watch you sleep
you're so peaceful
like art to my eyes
beautiful and delicate

PICTURE PERFECT

your love dawned on my soul
and woke me from the shadows

EPIPHANY

he asks me
what do you think
heaven's like

I place my hand
on his heart
and say
it's like this

HEAVEN

it's a beautiful thing
the moment you find love

I found it in your beautiful green eyes
that unforgettable night we spent on ocean drive

OCEAN DRIVE
(A POEM FOR OMAR SENAN)

up and down
round and round
this trip from reality
up here in the clouds
you're my best love yet
all my worries I'll forget
tell me what I want to hear
my mind's indefinitely set
take me far away
on a one way escapade
somewhere beyond the stars
cognitive foreplay
open my spiritual doors
got me on all fours
ready to make love to you
I'm forever yours

let me cut right to the chase
you and him could never compete
he's moving way too fast for you
and he's already stolen my heart
now he's on the run with it
and I love every moment of it
he does things you could never do
could you shake the earth
with your confidence in handling me
withstand the storms
make me feel like the empire state building
he makes me feel like the sh*t
and there ain't nothing he's lacking
his deep strokes
always have my waters trembling
and you never did get that deep
it's his profound ego
that has me tripping
I've fallen hard
and I ain't trying to get up

BOSS DADDY

his fingers
know how to work
every kink
out of my body

HE'S SO KINKY

you say
my body's
a delicacy
hope you're
hungry
don't starve
yourself
of what
your body
craves
so sweet
and juicy

bon appétit

tonight I'm going to entertain your deepest fantasies
show you what magic is really about

light every last candle in this house
and watch it burn down from the flames of our lustful desires

no need for you to hold back
tonight we're no longer slaves to the illusion of infatuation

I've waited too long for you on this tight rope walk of love
blindfolded by all these mixed emotions

allow me to levitate your senses to the highest level
I have powers you wouldn't even believe in

let your fingers be my first volunteer
as they work their way
from the arch of my back
down to center stage

then watch the rest of my clothes disappear
while this tongue performs tricks you've never seen

now for the best part of the show
the climax followed by an encore

let me slow it down this time
allow you the chance to catch your breath
as I hypnotize you to the sound of love

this is what magic is made of

THE MAGIC OF SEX

if I be your slave
promise me
your hands
will show me no mercy
let me crawl
and plead
at your feet
desperate to be consumed
I'm fifty shades deep
overstimulate me
intrigued
oozing with sexual creativity
lord you're so sexy
bound me with these ropes
tight grip around my throat
apply pressure right there
who cares – let them stare
foreplay magic
submission addict
full devotion
deliver on my word
soaking wet
like the ocean
come inside where it's warm
midnight entertainer
love to perform
full concentration
flip the switch
now beg for it

EROTICA

why are you
on your knees
begging for me
to show you mercy
when I'm already
halfway undressed
all of this wasted time
when you could've already been
halfway inside of me
fully swimming
in the deepest
bodies of my water
in these sensual rivers
that make up the being
you so desire
no need to ask for permission
drown in me
while I consume you whole
and let me bow
to honour you
face down
as my back end
rises to the occasion
my holy temple
yours for the taking
appreciate the fact that
there's no room in hell
for our sins
so instead we'll just
set this bed on fire
with the hours we spend
worshipping each other
the same way the sunflowers
worship the sun
we'll ignite an eternal flame
and cool it down from the sweat
that falls from our bodies
like rain from the sky
hydrating my cravings for you
I'll bless you
with all that I have
as we ride
into the sunset

HALFWAY INSIDE OF ME

let your love rain
down on these
crops of mine
this dry spell
love drought
crying out for the storm
some heavenly relief
bathe me in your sin

rain
till it can't rain no more

to let you
be inside of me
is not to fulfill a fantasy
it's to make a promise
between you and I

the promise of eternity

there are promises in your kisses
security in your touch
a passionate love story
in the way you look at me
I fall deeper and deeper
into your abyss
my poison of choice

there's no better way
to lose myself
than to lose myself to you

I BECOME A PART OF YOU

the angels sing
the oceans roar
the skies divide
the stars rejoice
while time stands still

every time we make love

I knew
I would fall quickly
for you

it was winter
the first time
we made love

when we finished
spring came calling

the flowers
instantly bloomed
and stood tall
to honour
the summer
of unconditional love
that followed

when we make love
I burn up inside
like an untamed fire

so gently you caress me
instantly I set ablaze

an inferno of passion and lust

ETERNAL FLAME

they came
in the mid of night
torches and pitch forks
calling out your name
threatening to burn
the entire house
to the ground
but I refused
to hand you over
so I held your hand
while we were engulfed
in flames

cause if we burn
we shall burn together

BURN TOGETHER

the day I have to
face this earth without you
is the day the earth
can take me back

let the soil deliver me
to your arms
let the flowers
that mark our grave
be a reminder that
true love existed here
my body next to yours
hand in hand
an undying love
a historical romance
even the children
will sing love songs
about our love story

THE DAY THE EARTH TOOK ME BACK

tell me
how can I stop
the hours from passing
the moon from rising
the sun from setting
the seasons from changing

I just want to be yours forever

FOREVER YOURS

you and I
like perfectly aged wine
paired with the right meal
intoxicated before
I even take a sip
I could drink you
down to the last drop

PERFECTLY AGED ROMANCE

the light of day
sometimes harsh
but time has a way
of healing all wounds

show me your scars
and I will free you
of your demons

drown your sins in lies
and our fortress shall sink

my forgiveness
becomes your sanctuary

your redemption
becomes my remedy

FORGIVENESS

I threw your heart into the ocean

if the tide shall return
it was meant to be

DESTINY

do you believe
in reincarnation

cause every time
we touch
I can feel
every love story
ever written in history

and could you possibly
believe in foreseeing
the future

cause every time
our eyes meet
I see you and I
together for eternity

and if you shall
ever leave
I strongly believe
that one day
you'll eventually
find your way
back to me

A LOVE STORY FOR THE AGES

if the trumpets shall sound
and the skies divide
it's you my love
that I will hold dearly
as I pray to the lord
to show us all mercy
while the golden gates open
for those who are righteous
together we'll ascended
or ascend not at all
cause there is no heaven
if heaven is without you

RAPTURE

I've dreamt so often that we would wed
on a beautiful june afternoon
while the hydrangeas dance and rejoice
to our eternal love that begins to bloom
hand in hand we'll confess our love
as white doves sing an everlasting tune
for now and forever, till death do us part
I'm yours I faithfully promise – I do

and as I wake from this blissful state
I pray that one day my dreams come true

A WEDDING IN JUNE

he cried
look at me
I have nothing left

I said
of course you do
you have me

even if we say goodbye
at least we got the chance
to know each other
not many people
can actually say
that in their lifetime
they were touched
by true love
so you'll always
be a part of me
cause the heart
never says farewell

YOU TOUCHED MY SOUL

after all is said and done
when the world grows tired
of believing in romance
and chivalry truly says its goodbyes
when the roses stop blooming
and love stories become a thing of the past
they will wonder how our love lasted the test of time

forever an eighth wonder of the world

EIGHTH WONDER OF THE WORLD

who could ever replace
you in my heart

this love we have
was eternally
engrave in my soul
from the moment we met

THERE'S NO REPLACEMENT

no relationship is perfect
but best believe
I'm perfectly in love with you

AND THAT'S ALL THAT MATTERS

if I was to open up
to you
and allow you to
see through my windows
and into my home
would you still
want to run your hands
through me
like running water
feel every inch
of my soul
know every room
in every corridor
and on my worst day
if I unlock
these doors
and allow you
to lay in my bed
would you rest peacefully
knowing the real me
or would you
repaint these walls
and turn
the lights off instead

someone once told me
if I stopped searching
and waited patiently
the love of my life
would come around

and it's true
cause years later
here I am
with you

LOVE OF MY LIFE

ACCEPTANCE

No matter how many times you change the exteriors
of your home, the interior memories and moments
can never be altered. The foundation of your home was
already built before you moved in. It's how you manage
your home that will reflect the owner within.

you cannot have me
nor can you break my spirit

the words leave my lips
as I draw back the curtains
and push open the window

I allow the night's breeze to hug my skin
watching the moon rejoice at the sight of me
it has longed to see my smile again
the feeling is mutual

I've spent many nights confined
to this prison I call a room
my bed an open casket
my happiness laid to rest

night after night
I drown myself in a sea of my emotions
but tonight is different

tonight I am blessed with an epiphany
touched by an angel
tonight I am not a slave to your lies
my shackles broken
tonight there is a light in me
that you can no longer diminish

for I've rebuked your curse
and now I am free

DEPRESSION

dear jona

time has escaped us
I hope you've been taking the time
to love yourself

there's something I have to confess
rainy days sometimes flood my mind of you
do you still think of me
the ghost of lovers' past
tell me, has your heart moved on
to a place far beyond haunted memories of
what we could have been
a world where I no longer exist
unable to torment you
with empty promises dressed in disappointment
a prisoner of emotional limbo

remember when you used to tell me
you were mine and I was yours for eternity
well I never got the chance to say *I'm sorry*

sorry for the hole I left in your expectations of me
never meant to tarnish the picture we promised to paint
my sweet gustav
I intended to cherish the kiss
but the colours bled too suddenly
leaving nothing but an empty canvas

if you're ever wondering about me
my spirit rests peacefully in the realization that
you can't hold onto what never
really belonged to you in the first place

and yes – I'm still trying to navigate
through this puzzle we call life
but no hard feelings my old friend

you've become one of the pieces to my journey
so I carry your heart close
and pray at night that it's my heart you carry
wherever you go

ETERNAL SUNSHINE OF A SPOTLESS MIND

the champion
is not the stronger competitor

the champion
is the one who finds victory
in every battle

even the ones lost

THE CHAMPION

I feel so connected to the galaxy
I'm more than just this mortal coil
somewhere floating in the stars
dipping through the milky way
endlessly searching for my sign

I must get this intellect from my AQUARIUS side
a thinker without boundaries upheld by pride
I haven't forgotten that the human condition doesn't come with ease
empathetic to the worlds growing pangs
and that I get from the PISCES
full of life and endless energy
always looking for a challenge like an ARIES
have patients with me sometimes you'll have to adjust
gets tough at times keeping up with a TAURUS
maybe I'm a GEMINI
on an adventure with my optimistic side
sometimes sensitive like a CANCER
spiritual conversations looking for all of life's answers
on the run from this generation's romance placebos
yearning to love and be loved like a LEO
or maybe the universe already had me at hello
just needed to be noticed and appreciated like a VIRGO
let my voice be of the peaceful LIBRA
my words harmonizing the world like an orchestra
life can be like a large casino
never afraid to gamble like the ambitious SCORPIO
I eat pray and love like a SAGITTARIUS
travelling through space and time in search of my happiness
against all odds one day I'll be reborn
if not today – tomorrow - the promise of a CAPRICORN

funny how the mind has the power to redefine
maybe the truth is that I'm each and every sign

ODE TO ASTROLOGY

misunderstood
frustrated
midnight cold sweats
why can't we all just get along
night ride on a highway to self-understanding
under the influence of creativity
fifty kilometers over life's limit
no time for meaningless life lessons
life's purpose on my mind
driven by social injustice
I'm here to leave an impact on your time
a deep spiritual connection to earth
controller of hate's demise
freethinker
truth seeker
rule breaker
I define the gravity within
friends come and go
internal anxiety stays forever
mistress to intuition
son of the moon
immortalities my gift
regulations in hot pursuit
so heavy on my spirit
why is the air so cold
minds constantly on fire
plummet off the halfway bridge
drowning in oppression
equality recession
isolation filling my lungs
communication with angels
resurface with purpose
on the run from myself
an endless battle
the thrill of evolution
not everyone can handle this pressure

INDIGO CHILD

first dates
like going to a masquerade ball

put on your best mask
to hide your flaws

dress to impress
to conceal your imperfections

but be wary
of who you choose
to portray
cause when
the clock strikes midnight
all truths are revealed

I gave myself away to the night
and when the sun rose that morning
I had to face the day

THE SEED YOU SOW IS THE SEED YOU REAP

forget about guns and fists
do not allow violence to control you
instead allow your words and wisdom
to hit them where it hurts

why are we
always trying to change
winter into spring
summer into fall
night into day
the minutes into hours

let things happen naturally

AN ODE TO
BARBARA HARRIS' LECTURES

the feeling of loneliness
fled my being
the very moment
I came to realize
the importance of
family

I moved to the city
to get away from home
start a life of my own
but everything's so loud here
nobody pays attention to me
and the fire engines
remind me how much
I miss the country
my family
and home

HOME IS WHERE THE HEART IS

where's the love
we're going back
barely forth
family dinners
barely anyone there
what happened to
family first
the enemies attacking
and it's defense we're lacking
our empire
overthrown by our differences
barely recognized you there
weren't we raised
under the same roof
holidays
the only time I see all of you
death in the family
only time we see
the importance
of family through
church on sundays
praying for forgiveness
for messing up mother's vision
sister's distant
her heart moved on
to her replacement kin
stories true
maybe if we were there for one another
brother wouldn't be
going to jail to pay his dues
father wants us to try to connect
his bloodline's bleeding through
descendants of a common ancestry
become strewed
nana still waiting for a visit
with hopes I'll pass through

but I'm still sitting here
wondering when
this reality show will debut
will it finally open our eyes to reality
wonder if they'll call it family feud

FAMILY FEUD

find the time to spend with
the ones you love

regret has a way of
reminding us
that time is irreversible

REGRET

father's been laid off
mother's starving to feed us
brother's selling drugs to make ends meet
I've been singing the melody of rent past due
yet we're all still dancing in celebration to life's tune

THE WORLD CONTINUES WITH OR WITHOUT YOU

it was early dawn
when my father
woke me from my slumber
and led me
out into the woods

he told me
we were going out hunting
for the meaning of adulthood

as the eldest
he told me
it was my duty
to bring back
foods of wisdom
to ripen the minds
of my siblings
who would soon
follow in my footsteps

he warned me
that there was no sleep
for the soul in this lifetime

and as I held his gun high
he told me to shoot
for a better life
than he ever had

so I aimed
to prove to him
that I was worthy
of his lessons
in becoming a man

FATHERS' LESSONS

my father was a man
who was handed a toolbox
from his father when he was just a boy
but this toolbox had no tools inside

so tell me

how could we ever blame him
for not building the perfect home
without having the right tools

THE EMPTY TOOLBOX

Forged out of love, my mother was my favorite
weapon in battle against life:

1. She was sharper than the sharpest blade.
    She taught me what it meant to have a swift and
    discerning intellect.

    Always two steps ahead of the enemy

2. She was light to handle even in the worse
    of storms. I always found a way to appreciate
    the lesson at hand to understand her true intentions.

    My victory

3. There was never a day that passed that she wasn't
    by my side. I always held her close. She gave me
    exactly what I needed.

    Security

4. When the enemy drew close and all hope seemed
    lost, I looked up to her for guidance. She believed
    in me the way I believed in her. She reminded me
    that I would make it through.

    My reassurance

5. When the enemy struck, they were no match
    for a warrior like me. Minds impure, armor of
    hate and tongues as venomous as a king cobra.
    Their weapons could never pierce my heart.
    A shield like no other.

    The strength and wisdom that ran through my blood

6. Even though the days grow old and I am much
    older now, she remains close to my heart.
    Forever a reminder of how I became...

    The king that I am

THE KINGDOM WITHIN YOUR MOTHER

sometimes I wonder
what my mother's life
would have been like if
she never had me at sixteen

would she be happier
possibly more alive

would she be living her
version of the perfect life
or maybe even feel complete
having achieved her dreams

I guess we'll never know

what I do know is that I'm
grateful that she sacrificed
everything to keep me

and I just hope that
I've made her proud enough
in this life to fill that void of
what if

MY MOTHER'S SACRIFICE

the moment I was born
my mother held me in her arms and smiled

looking down at me with great joy
she knew that I was delivered to do great things

and great things I shall do

POEM FOR MY MOTHER

my mother had me at sixteen
she lived sixteen different lives
just to give us a better one

now I will live sixteen different lives
to give her the world back sixteen fold

GIVE BACK TO THOSE WHO GIVE TO YOU

someone once told me
super heroes are figments of our imaginations

guess they never met my mother

THE WOMAN OF MANY POWERS

what gift could ever be better
than the gift of life

thank you mom and dad

when I have a child
I am going to nourish him
the way my grandmother nourished me

I will bathe him in love
feed him encouragement
and wipe away his tears
with promises of a bright future

THE DAY I HAVE A CHILD

I regret the day
you left home
never to come back
resting your spirit
in a new place
of white lights
and eternal peace
and here I stand
alone with nothing
but time
trying to find
all the right ways
to say goodbye
but it's too late
and how I wish
I could reverse time
and apologize
for all the times
I took you for granted
and granted
we all get caught up
in this busy life
you'll forever be
on my mind
there's where I'll
keep memories of you
revisiting them time to time
with hopes one day
we'll reunite
and look back and laugh
at all of the moments we shared

CHERISH THE DAY

do not take the fruits of my tree
if your intentions are not to replant their seeds

THE TREE OF KNOWLEDGE OF GOOD AND EVIL

my art is not the written word
my art is the essence of who I am
open to interpretation
closed to hate
not everyone will support my work
and that I am understanding of
but my work has no room for negativity
for I am the keeper of peace

PEACEKEEPER

I want each and every word
that escapes my mouth
to be stepping stones
towards greatness
for those that come after me

CHILDREN OF THE FUTURE

I want my art
to be a lighthouse
to those in search
of shelter
the words
on these pages
a beacon
for the lost

LIGHTHOUSE

this world is crazy
and every day
I'm fighting
for my sanity
it's this generation
that's sick
diagnosed with a need for
materialistic sh*t
it's extremely contagious
and unfortunately we've
all caught it

OUTBREAK OF MADNESS

taking the easy way out
is called the easy way for a reason
I could have been
the accessory on some
older gentleman's arm
to reap the reward
of bloodied money
or have been
an open tunnel
for men looking to travel
to and from their sexual fantasies
just for the taste of
materialistic things
but instead
after all these years
of hard work
long nights
and the breakdowns
achieving success
from these hands
brings my soul
deep satisfaction
and that you can't get
from the easy way out

THE EASY WAY OUT

I've seen money
turn the gentlest of men
into savage beasts

ROOT OF ALL EVIL

sometimes I hear the wilderness
call out to me as if somehow deep within
lays a beast anxious to be set free
a beast drawn to the darkness of the shadows
the collector of sins with a hunger for self-pleasures
but my god has warned me of this beast
stepping into the wild will only draw spirits
for these spirits find amusement in feeding the beast
I long to comprehend my desires to face such a creature
when I am a man that belongs to none that stand with the wicked
who has sworn to live in the temple of righteousness all his days
yet a connection so strong I cannot shake
has me up pacing in my chambers in the mid of night
calling out to the beast to set me free
to share my light in the darkness of his dwelling
an unbreakable bond linked for eternity

THE BEAST AND THE WILDERNESS

if the devil wears prada
I'll take three
what's there to fear
if suppression is the real nightmare
and if I grind hard enough
I'll be able to live the american dream
a slave to the spotlight
whatever you need me to be
lies become a place of rest for reality
I grow tired of what I should be
slave to the rules of society
prisoner to materialistic things
let me drip of sexuality
stars in my eyes and money on my mind
I'll kill whoever stands in the way
cause I'm tired of this nine to five
haven't really ever felt alive
until I let the need for power inside
countless sleepless nights
slowly losing my mind
everyone has a little Andrew Cunanan inside

ANDREW CUNANAN

break on through
these emotions
that hold you
back from me

until then
I'll be here waiting
for you
in lovers' purgatory

we may not be
the same in nature
or always agree
but when we compromise
sunshowers follow

emotionally lost in translation
most complicated puzzle
a hurricane in the morning
gentle breeze by night fall
and yet despite it all
in your eyes I'm just a
beautiful disaster

BEAUTIFUL DISASTER

I'm a silent storm
that not many men
have the power
to weather

SILENT STORM

follow me
into the dark deep
your emotions
my harp
let me play from your
heart strings
an enchanted melody
and you'll follow
freely
cause as much
as you deny
yourself the truth
you love
the darkest
parts of me

SIREN

the modern day love story
a dysfunctional romantic tale
starring everything about your relationship
directed by today's generation
playing on all social media near you

ROMANCE COMEDY OF THE YEAR

when you're gone
I miss you

when you're here
I long to miss you

is any of it really worth it

the arguments
the distance
the pettiness

what if something happened
and you were no longer here

who would I
share my world with
kiss goodnight
wake up next to

let's not forget
the present
is a gift

THE PRESENT IS A GIFT

I complain
about men
coming and going
loving me
and then
not loving me enough
and then here I am
some days loving myself
and others not

HYPOCRITE

the ones that
speak ill of you
and curse your name
are the ones you must
pray for and bless more

I'm always searching
for myself
constantly growing
a cycle with
no means to and end
for the end only means
the end of my journey

picture a world
where we are
side by side
hand in hand
blessing one another
as we gratefully
give back
to the earth
in which we take from

THANKSGIVING

when my time comes
and I have to go
heavenly father I pray
you come
and carry me home

I just want to
thank God
for allowing me
to be here
to share
my journey
and hopefully
my voice
will represent
those
silently
crying out
to be heard

SINCERELY

In the beginning God created the heavens and the earth.
Before there was light, there was darkness. Before there was agony, there was Elaine.

Now, she was the most graceful angel sent down from the heavens. Sent down to remind us that everyone is worthy of forgiveness.

When God delivered her to the first home, he told her to act human – to rest, eat, pray and live as a child. So, she did as told. She was innocent, she could do no wrong, but with innocence and purity closely follows evil. The father of the house grew jealous of her divine happiness so he clipped her wings. Took away what made her special, and with that she became tainted. Flooded with human emotions - hate, rage, sorrow, regret – all at once. She became human. Unable to ascend back home; back to the light she once held in her heart.

With the years that passed, she tried to make the best out of the life she was given. She gave birth to a beautiful daughter who later breathed life into her grandchildren that would ultimately continue her legacy.

Life wasn't always easy for her. The longer she was here, the more human she became. She came to experience loss and grief. The emptiness inside her opened doors to the wicked ways of this earth. Slowly corrupting the spirit within.

It wasn't until she found her faith again that she found herself. God had been waiting for her at the river with open arms and the promise of redemption. He told her to wash her feet of exhaustion, to feed her spirit with hope, to allow family to heal her scars and to build the strength to repair her wings.

Before he left, he placed his hand on her right cheek and looked
into her shallow eyes before telling her that heaven can barely
wait for her glorious return. That the other angels have been
watching her throughout her entire journey and are so proud of
her accomplishments on this earth.

As he began to ascend, he kissed her on the cheek and said
peace and forgiveness can only be found within
and with that he vanished,
leaving her here to finish her work
to leave her mark on this earth.

in hardship or turmoil
when you face
the darkest moments in your life
search deep within
that's where you'll find Saint Elaine

SAINT ELAINE

as I weep on the pages of King James
the Lord's ears open and I pray:

for me
for all that I have done
for the people I have let down
for my sanity
for a cure for loneliness
for eternal love
for my happiness
for redemption
for peace within
for stability
for somewhere to call home
for forgiveness
for a family of my own
for purpose
for the career of my dreams
for the world to come together
for racism to end
for hate to bloom into love
for the wicked to fall to their knees
for more women in power
for equal rights

and at the end of it all
I pray I find myself

POWER OF PRAYER

PEACE

You must first throw all of your hard work into your fireplace and relax as your troubles burn away, covering you in warmth. It's not until you let go, that you will finally come to realize how peaceful your lovely home is.

the world pressed the palm of its
hand against my chest and the air
from my ancestors escaped my
lungs

the pain was insufferable so I
cried out the river my father
taught me to drink from

and in that I disappointed the
blood that ran through my veins
which fed the image representing
the blessings I belonged to

I even changed my last name to
make myself feel a little
less than who I really was

I told myself that I could never be crowned
as the knight in white armor because
I was plagued with black roots that ran
so deep

enraged I ripped out the weeds that grew from the
garden on my head to hide the fact
that a tiger cannot change his stripes

will my soul ever find its way home

STRIPES OF A TIGER

my whole life
I've walked around
with this suitcase
my ancestors
passed down to me

I've always complained
about these
hand me downs
instead of changing
my old torn rags

foolish me

how I could have gone
from rags to riches

RAGS TO RICHES

little black boy
you are a blessing to this world
you will do extraordinary things
you are the change we are praying for
don't let the lies of society mislead your spirit
you are not the product of hate
nor are you a generational curse
created by simple minded men
there is more to your core
than the color of your skin
you are rich in culture
highly educated
beautiful at best
you can be whatever you set your mind to
you are the promises of promises
this I want you to never forget

LITTLE BLACK BOY

have you ever seen a sight as beautiful
as the african daisies that bloom so gracefully
the moment spring comes knocking

what about the ambitious bees that never sleep
who sing songs about nights forever long

or the breadfruit that hangs high in the caribbean trees
full of culture and history

those lucky to see a sight that stood the tests of time
like the imperial palace in the home to those eritrean queens

there's a humbling picture to see
of families fighting for survival in somalia's streets

it's the beauty and essence of a black woman
that our eyes sometimes are not open to see

ESSENCE OF A BLACK WOMAN

2 cups of brown sugar

¼ cup of caramel

1 table spoon of honey

4 dark chocolate squares

a pinch of nutmeg

a dash of cocoa

¾ cups of pecans

a few pralines

mix them together and
this is how you create the beauty
of the black community

A RECIPE FOR BLACK BEAUTY

celebrate your culture
like every day is carnival

jerk chicken
family summer barbecues
dad yelling at us for playing too much
church on sundays
prayer before dinner
ackee picking in grandma's backyard
long autumn drives to new york
aunts vibrantly gossiping
mother braiding sister's hair in the back
cod liver oil and cocoa butter
lessons on how not to burn plantain
fubu and rocawear tracksuits

this is the culture I grew to love and know

NOSTALGIA

sisters plotting against sisters
brothers killing brothers

how can we call ourselves a community
when we are constantly at war with one another
giving the real enemy exactly what they want

A FOOLS WAR

this hair
that grows
on my head
is the crown
I gracefully wear
passed on to me
by my people
who sacrificed
their lives
through slavery
so that
their descendants
could be
future kings
and queens

KINGS & QUEENS

you tried to divide
you tried to conquer
you tried to deprive

hand in hand
side by side
connection of great minds
hearts aligned
with time we became wise
you won't win this time

STRENGTH IN NUMBERS

you tried to purify
me in the rivers
of your society
but you cannot
purify what is
already cleansed
within

PURITY

gently on my toes
I float like a butterfly
degrade my ethnicity
and I'll sting like a bee
go ahead if you're brave
I dare you - test me
I'll gladly school you on
the importance of equality
me versus illiberality
I'll go all fifteen rounds
like Muhammad Ali

MUHAMMAD ALI

every night I have the same dream...

I close my eyes and see a day when the world
decides to host the biggest dinner party and at that party
there's one representative from each contemporary
ethnic group claiming their seat at earths table.

they eat, drink, laugh and shares gifts from their cultures.

they celebrate unity and peace long into the night and in
the morning, they return home to their land to share
the cultural gifts they were each blessed with.

THE DREAM OF UNITY

the rich culture and colorful history that
drips from your melanin was painted by the
blood, sweat and tears of your ancestors

we are their everlasting masterpiece

I used to stare at myself in the mirror
wondering why god created me the way he did

skin brown like caramel
hair wild like an untamed garden of herbs
body imperfect like unripe fruit

I used to resent the reflection staring back at me
then I realized...

what I thought were flaws
were actually ingredients he purposely chose
a recipe perfect in his image

PERFECT IN HIS IMAGE

they tell us that being black isn't good enough
that we need to look more european
perm and relax our hair
when truly it's ya'll that need to relax on all of that
afros are not meant for the workplace
and that the black man should never lead - only follow
but really what are you trying to say to us
Martin Luther King, Rosa Parks and Malcom X
were they not leaders against the tide
and are we not the heirs of their hard earned fortunes
or are we just children stripped from their kin against our own will
yes we are worthy of leading roles
and front page spreads in magazines
after all is it not our full lips and chestnut skin that you so desire
black history month is the one shortest month out of the year
the other eleven are textbooks lined with the white man's history
so help us understand why Kunta Kinte becomes the butt of a joke
and who we should all strive to be is James Dean or Marilyn Monroe
they say slavery ended in the eighteen sixty five but if that's true
why are we still fighting for a spot on the porch

BLACK HISTORY MONTH

I will not go gently
let them wage war
obviously the world hasn't evolved
we've just slowed down
negativity in the air
who are they to tell us
men can only love women
and that women solely belong to men
heart of equality
mind of rebellion
destroy all bridges for us to cross
and we will march through this stagnant river
through the storm of separation
let me through
let me face the simple minded
and when they curse me with hate
I will spit peace in the face of ignorance
they will come to learn the hard way
that the power of hate will never break us down

REVOLUTION

remember the moment
I told you I was into men
you threw stones at my spirit
burned it down like Sodom and Gomorrah
and there I was alone in the cold
dressed in the scriptures of Mary Magdalene
praying for the world to forgive me
for being born plagued in your eyes

it must have been the passage of Isaac and Abraham
that brought you to your knees in the mid of night
unable to fathom the thought
of a father sacrificing his own son

haunting visions of a boy crying out
to his father only to be slaughtered on
an altar of ignorance

but love is unconditional
and forgiveness is the promise of our lord
for he who is conditioned can be unconditioned

so patience became our new found faith and testimony
a relation of many blessings for years to come

now each morning I rejoice in your name my father
as I listen to you sing my name to him most highest
while the angels weep in joy
celebrating the beauty of a father's love for his son

selah!

THE PASSAGE OF ABRAHAM
FATHER OF ISAAC

I was thrown
into a pit of
black mambas
and came out
the only one alive

if your attempt
is to poison my mind
and crush my spirit
you're going to
have to try
a little harder
than that

PIT OF BULLIES

these stretch marks
represent the
stretch in distance
it took me
to run
this confidence
into first place
so don't
cheat me of
natural beauty
with your lines
of judgement

my tattoos
are not a disgrace
to my beautiful skin
they are the story
that completes
the beauty within

TATTOO

trust me
I know you're exhausted
but if you were to leave
where would you go
where would you stay
the world would break
like all the hearts
of your loved ones
and this earth
needs you
like the oceans
need rain
so if you just hold on
a little longer
I promise you
you'll get stronger
time will heal the pain
and even though
we don't know
each other
we're both human
we're the same
and sometimes
I feel what you feel
don't feel alone
don't let the troubles
of this world erase
your god given name
we can't afford
to lose another angel
please I beg you
just stay

SUICIDE NOTE

whoever told you that you were worthless
was probably told that they were worthless
by someone who felt worthless

hate is contagious
stop the spread of this disease
and let love be the cure

say it
I am worthy

I AM WORTHY

every day I shed my problems
like the skin of a snake
leaving my worries behind
like the way I left behind
yesterday

they broke you down
took from every part of you
yet you are still here

you are the testimony
of mental strength
and emotional endurance

STRENGTH AND ENDURANCE

with his hand around my neck he says to me
you talk too much for your own good
maybe you should learn to speak only when spoken to

I laugh at him as I break through his grip
does independence speak only when communism tells it to

LAW OF INDEPENDENCE

holding me back
will only do you more damage
in the end

look what happens when
a lion is held back
from the wild

can we actually fly
if the skies the limit

does the galaxy have room for me
with all the stars
flashing lights
and fancy cars

am I really one
in a million
if the world consists
of over a billion

are my prayers overheard
when sometimes I choose to be
ignorant to the word

guess I'm still searching
trying to figure out
where I belong

YEARNING TO BELONG

lately
I've been trying
to get to know me
and I've tuned out
everything else
so now
I can finally
hear myself

LISTEN TO YOURSELF

who's to say I'm not a king
if I rule the emotions of
this kingdom within

you love it when
I strip down to nothing but my core
as I stimulate you with my intellect

and you know I love it when
you enter my deepest values
and penetrate me with your integrity
as I scream out for more

THE ATTRACTION OF SUBSTANCE

the older boys with experience
used to tell me

when life gives you lemons
you make the perfect tea that no
man could ever resist

so with time I grew into the largest tree in town
that bore the most desirable lemons

my years of patience brought experienced
sugar and perfectly aged honey

and boy let me tell you
there's nothing sweeter
than my sugar honey ice tea

SUGAR HONEY ICE TEA

pain is just an illusion
of the mind

for I am the illusionist
who controls the show

THE ILLUSION OF PAIN

dear side man/side chick

this one goes out to you

I bet you thought you demolished
the foundation we built
the deep connection I painted within him
did you think you renovated our home
changed the blue print
from under my feet
guess again
love and redemption
will always be stronger
than the distasteful class
and deceiving tools
of a dehydrated
door to door
salesman
looking to sell
a handful of cheap tricks
to naïve buyers
and yes you have the receipts
of his purchases
but I issue the invoices
that keep the lights on
and the water running
so laugh it up
while you can
cause in time
these broken windows
will be fixed
the locks will be changed
and your stench
will be gone for good

so feel free to move on
cause he no longer
needs your services

yours truly,

his forever home

HOME RENOVATIONS

I no longer cry at night
when I think of you

those tears became my testimony
a reminder of why I'm better off without you

TESTIMONY OF TEARS

the powerful and beautiful
butterfly I've become
as I emerge
from the cocoon of uncertainty
to find peace of mind

I am finally free
from your stronghold
an alluring sight to see

METAMORPHOSIS OF FREEDOM

my mind and soul
now orchestrators
of their own
a beautiful melody
they now sing

THE SYMPHONY OF EMANCIPATION

today
I celebrate the death
of what we once had
I'll be dancing in the streets
saying goodbye to you
and my mother told me
I shouldn't mourn the dead
that I should enjoy
the release from limbo instead
so I'll be dressed in the
moments we shared
to remind myself
that there's better
for me out there

DAY OF THE DEAD

the moment I came out to the world
was the moment I began living

coming out isn't easy
trust me
I know

all of the lonely nights
contemplating whether
I was worthy of life or not
all those days I spent
pretending to be
someone I was not

the spirit cracks
under such pressure

I can't lie to you
and tell you that
life will be perfect
or that
each and every person
will accept you
with open arms

but I can confidently
tell you
that there is nothing
wrong with you

if the world
is not willing
to accept you
for you
then that is
their loss

there is a community
waiting to embrace you
waiting to free you
from the exile you feel

DON'T BE AFRAID TO LIVE FOR YOURSELF

the old me
died today
there will be a
new me tomorrow
and a newer me
the day after that

close your eyes
rest easy my old friend
cause even in your last moments
I will be here
to hold your hand
and guide you back home
lean on me
and worry no more
for your work here is done
so let your spirit
be at ease
cause I know
you've been home sick
and don't worry about me
I'll heal in time
and I promise you
one day
we will meet again

PEOPLE HELP THE PEOPLE

the world
sadly whispered
goodbye
as I laid there
bleeding out
alone
that cold
september night
on the ground
in front of
the barber shop
where I had just
fallen victim
to the bullet
of a gun
that was loaded
for another man
a man
who took life
for granted
but I guess
I might as well
have been the target
since I too
never appreciated
the gift of life
the sky dimmed
as I begged
the lord for mercy
to prove
worthy of the privilege
to enjoy his reward

so I prayed
for more time to
fix my wrongs
to find salvation
and be there for
my little sister
cause I need her
more than she thinks
so god heard my cries
and told me to rise
and so I rose

AS I LAY HERE DYING
(SEPTEMBER 24, 2013)

I never got
the chance
to thank you
for all the pain
and heartache
and lately
I've been loving
the brand new me
it took me awhile
but eventually
I broke right on through
so thanks
cause I couldn't have
done it
without you

REBIRTH

first comes the hurting
then comes the burning pain
the promise of heartache
but I promise you
like a phoenix
you shall
rise from the ashes

FROM THE ASHES YOU SHALL RISE

ridicule my hair
mock my culture
hate on the colour
of my skin

these are the things
that make me content

the joke is on you
my friend

TO LOVE YOURSELF IS A THING OF BEAUTY

take great care of your soulmate
feed them well
nourish their soul with love
treat them here and there
please them sexually
take them to fancy places
remind them how beautiful they are

now stand in front of the mirror
and remind yourself what your
soulmate looks like

SOULMATE

I have the strength
to lift this world up
with positivity

the stamina to run
for miles to catch
my dreams

the power inside
to make a difference

the courage
to overcome any
form of negativity

and there's nothing
that can stop me

because change
begins within me

IT BEGINS WITHIN ME

my biggest regret
was sitting around
waiting for the world
to tell me
when it was okay
to catch my dreams
and now that
I'm chasing them
I couldn't be
happier

YOU HAVE THE RIGHT TO DREAM

he tells me
I'll never
find better

fact is
I've already found better

I've found myself

when the sun
crawled into the sky
I came knocking
at the palace
of acceptance
naked and exposed
I was starving
so I begged for love
and purpose
but my cries
were not heard
nobody came
to my rescue
so I ran
in desperation
to the end
of the world
to find myself again
and when
I got there
the wind spoke
into my lungs
filling my heart
with completeness
she told me
that the greatest love of all
comes from within
and with her words
I built a palace of my own

ODE TO GREATEST LOVE OF ALL
BY WHITNEY HOUSTON

I used to think heaven
was a place above the clouds
that was until I found peace of mind
and learned how to love myself

that is where I found heaven

THE PATH TO HEAVEN

the storm
will destroy
your sacred land
take your crops
and kill the livestock
you put all of
your hard work into
but believe me
stand strong
because after
every disaster
with time
there is room
to repair
for the sun
has been waiting
to see
your smile again

AFTER THE STORM

the audience claps
I bow
feeling complete
the curtains lower

this is my art

my feelings
the show in which
I hope you enjoyed

THE ART OF FEELING

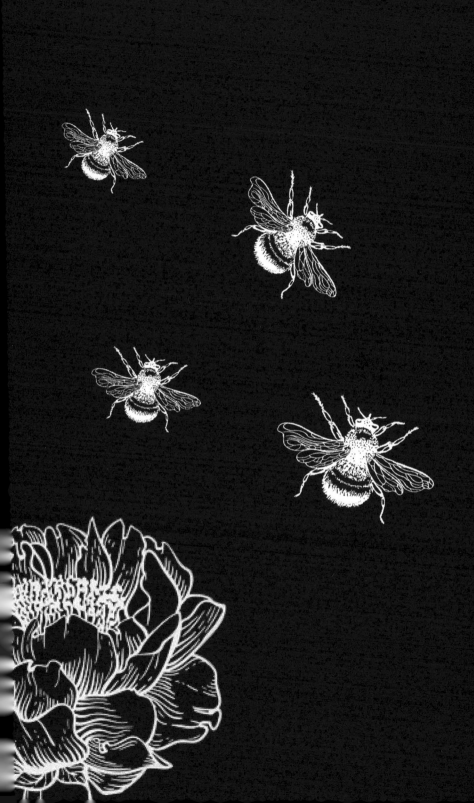

you have reached the end of our journey

I pray that somewhere along the path you were able to
find peace within and the closure that you deserve

I cannot thank you enough
for allowing me to share twenty eight years
of sorrow, love, acceptance and peace
please never hesitate
to share my remedy and always take
as much as you need
the world can be greedy at times
but rest assured that nobody
will ever be able to take
the essence of these poems
away from you
and remember
when the heart aches
when you're full of joy
or unsure of it all
wrap your wounds
and accomplishments
with these pages
all will be okay
when you come
to understand
the art of feeling

you tell me to tell you about myself
so I open the front door:

I've always been a house to scattered emotions

a bed with wrinkled sheets
a kitchen with food to share
a bathroom for peoples' sh*t
a hidden closet - once closed now open
a guest room for friends to rest
a never ending hallway searching for life's answers
a living room waiting to join family
a bedroom to make love
a staircase leading to inner peace
an attic of stored knowledge
a window with an open view
a misunderstood den
a basement with dark secrets

but this is my house
and I wouldn't change it
for the world
but what I can do is
leave on the lights for you

the art of feeling is a collection
of poetry about
embracing love
finding peace
overcoming heartache
appreciating life
letting go
and moving on
each chapter is
designed to
guide the reader
to understand
what it means
to feel
and the art
behind the gift
of feeling

Made in the USA
Middletown, DE
02 June 2021

40856345R00124